FEATHERS
IN THE
MIST

WISPERINGS OF
LOVE AND HOPE

T.B HUMAN

Published by TRUITY AUSTRALIA™

Copyright © 2017   T.B. HUMAN ™

Paper Back   ISBN-13: 978-1-876776-09-1

All rights reserved. No part of this book may be reproduced or transmitted in any form or by any means, electronic or mechanical, including photocopying, recording, or by any information storage and retrieval system, without permission in writing from the copyright owner.

While this is a true narrative, names and places have been changed to protect the identity of those involved.

First published 1999 revised 2017 and republished.

www.authortbhuman.com

To the Reader:

To everyone who has ever searched for meaning,
may these words lift your spirit and heal your soul.

Wisdom is something often seen as
illusive, one moment you think you have
it and the next it is gone again,

Catching wisdom is like catching
"Feathers in the Mist"

To use this little book, simply hold a question
in your mind and then open the book to
where your spirit takes you for inspiration.

Many Blessing

God's blessings to you great one.

Come journey home with me,

Hold my hand and walk beside me as a friend.

I will be with you always,

In thoughts, in dreams,

in life's every breath,

And in death I will walk you through the door.

This I promise-

May grace be with you all days of your life

I love you dear friend-

Believe this.

FEATHERS IN THE MIST

Birds take flight upon silent wings
Soaring high towards the morning sun
Each alone, but together.

So, it should be with you little one,
walk on your own two feet
No need to lean on anyone.
There will be times you need to
rest, and place your head
On a caring chest.
Gather to yourself the wisdom,
bring your heart a brighter truth
Catch the feathers in the mist and
these will lead you home.

Mists rise with the early morning sun,

Soon the mists will disappear

A time of laughter no more tears

Gather to your heart the understanding,

Recognize the truth somehow,

Know the power of your thoughts

And build world that is full and bright

Build it now with all your might

And lead the world with shining light.

Question: How do we escape from the pains of what we experience in this world?

Answer: It is only within the stillness that we combine with the source of all things and become at peace and at one For all time.

Peace be with you child of light,

The dove flies over the horizon,

In search of new lands,

Behold, it carries a sprig of spruce,

To show there is a future.

FEATHERS IN THE MIST

My love,

Feelings remembered,

Stirred deep inside,

A longing no one else will ever fill.

Emptiness, so desolate it is death.

But in death, comes rebirth.

A time free of such longings, forever more.

Once more to feel complete, within the purpose.

Journeys end is near

Soon we will meet once more

In life as in death separated never more.

When thoughts run wild and confusion

fills the mind remember

"I am not confused

I am just changing"

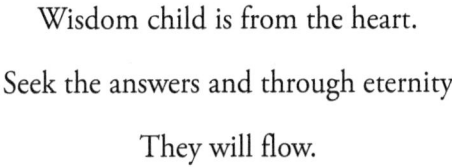

Wisdom child is from the heart.

Seek the answers and through eternity

They will flow.

Why let other people's thoughts

cloud and confuse you

Truth is something deep inside,

It is what you know – without knowing how or why

You are simply testing your truth.

Love is the reflection

Of the person

I seek to become

I love you dear friend.

FEATHERS IN THE MIST

My love, do not fear,

For you know I am very near.

In all things we will be put to task

Be positive and calm is all we ask.

Remember, today is a brand-new day

In which to run and to play.

Keep light heart and free,

For we keep the best for thee.

Others now may be unkind,

As their feelings do unwind

Pass it through do not absorb the pain,

Do not let your journey be in vain.

For in time the truth is all that will remain.

T.B. HUMAN

Once so low I could not stand,

For I had built my home on sand.

Blown to the wind with each new dawn,

Each time the search would end just torn.

Till a secret whispered by the son,

One early morn as it begun.

Look to your heart and find the key,

a better life for your there will be.

So, I turned to face my heart within,

And found it shattered, flung upon the wind.

How do I find the missing links?

Acceptance will replace the chinks.

Accepting that I am me,

And there's no one else I'd rather be.

So gently, I began the search.

Inside, oh God how much it hurts!

FEATHERS IN THE MIST

With each old pain unveiled within,

Came torment, pain, finally understanding.

Finally, the veil of darkness is growing thin,

The light at last is shining in.

With each new day I feel the glow,

Ever stronger, stronger, I will grow.

Until one day I will be free, of what

everyone else expects of me.

True wealth is happiness of the soul.

This can not be measured,

Stored, hoarded or stolen,

Unless we allow it to be.

Be happy little one,

Let you joy fill the universe with light,

So, all may see and follow,

Without you saying one single word.

Just by being.

No one can ever know the loneliness of the night

Greater than one who has lost their self.

Sing a song of times ago,

Sing a song of tales of woe,

Sing a song of truth and gallant knights,

Sing a song again we will win the fight.

For all in strength our souls to win,

And never more our souls to sin.

Bring us now a gentle lamb,

For in his hands our lives truly stand

FOR DAYS OF TROUBLE.

All is well,

In it's right place at this time,

I have no fear; I release it all to God,

I am where I should be,

And have the strength and confidence,

To carry out all that I am needed to accomplish,

I am what I should be,

I know my burden is no heavier than I can carry,

For this day.

I go where I am needed, in the faith of god,

My pathway is guided by his hand,

All is well.

May my path be clearly shown to me,

And I will follow without question.

All is well.

I seek the perfect calm of god,

And rest in his constant love and guidance,

May I reflect always calm peace and love.

Always when I am troubled let me return,

To this perfect peace of all that is,

All is well.

Caresses, caresses but touch me not,

My heart is sealed in a stone.

Chains bind me to this earthly plain forever,

And time runs on forever.

Give me time dear lass, forever,

Please, time is all I ask,

For all things will come to pass.

Once more to be together,

Within love that lasts forever.

Why the fear of me why the pain?

My love for you is strong,

Summer comes again.

T.B. HUMAN

You are only ever protected from your own will,

And often it's your own will which

causes you the trouble.

FEATHERS IN THE MIST

Gentle blessings from above,

Flow on now to my true love.

Flow now from deep within,

A time for inner questioning.

A time to know all that we do,

Will bring Gods blessings flowing through.

Allow his light to shine through you,

And know his love in all you do.

Be sure his strength will help your fight,

For he gives freely with all his might.

To every soul who hears his call,

Answers come to one and all.

The call to peace, the call to love,

Clear all old debts, is the message now from above.

Now there is no time to waste,

As each day we strive to win the race.

T.B. HUMAN

The race for good and love and light,

Reach now my love with all your might.

Be sure my angels are standing near,

And your calls for help they truly hear.

They light your path with hope not fear,

And not one of you need shed a tear.

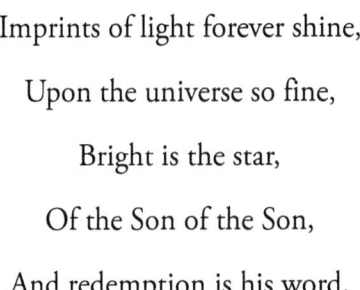

Imprints of light forever shine,

Upon the universe so fine,

Bright is the star,

Of the Son of the Son,

And redemption is his word.

T.B. HUMAN

Gazing through the window pane,

I sit silently and watch the rain,

I see the gifts God brings in tears

I think of all the wasted years.

Then a voice inside me cries,

For all the heartache,

All the lies.

All for a purpose I am told,

Heartache is the way to gold.

Gold of spirit

Gold of truth.

Pain is just a tool to grow,

To find the truth you seek to know.

First find, what is not truth within,

And then will come the understanding.

Truth is a feeling of Joy inside,

Joy of Spirit soaring high,

Shining out for all to see,

Happiness finds truth,

Can't you see?

When wracked with pain it simply is,

Spirit telling us we are out of touch.

For God is Joy and Abundance too,

May his blessings flow to you.

In every thought and action too.

T.B. HUMAN

My love, do not fear,

For you know I'm very near.

In all things we must be put to task,

Be positive and calm is all we ask.

Remember, today is a brand-new day,

In which to run and then to play.

Keep light heart and free,

For we keep the best for thee.

Others now may be unkind,

As their feelings do unwind.

Pass it through do not absorb the pain.

Pass it through to those who wait,

Forever ready at God's golden gate.

Heart stills its cry,

I awake from the darkness of the night,

A new day full of adventures,

I know somewhere in time,

We are one.

Only to hold on to that sense of knowing,

It brings such peace.

It is, I am, we are, One.

As I come to the core of my being,

As I search for my truth

I understand how individual and precious

I truly am.

Decisions made beyond this time

Many lives I've left behind

Distant Memories, just traces

Glimpses of unknown faces

Dreams of other times I now recall

What is the meaning of it all?

Shadows of a lifetime reflect upon my world,

Each perception,

Each encounter,

Challenging growth, challenging old ways

Will I anger at the injustice?

Or will I grow letting go of the old seeking

always further understanding?

God's gifts are opening to you,

Allow them to flow,

Set your light high, at full beam.

Be master of your own boat,

Know your destination.

Be it truth,

Be it self.

Know the seas of discontent,

How they whip up wild storms.

Recognize this.

Do not allow this to be,

Reach to the heavens for answers,

And they will be given.

In time,

All will come in time.

You are the child,

And the father showers his blessings upon you.

The illusion would be that you not see them,

For what they truly are, Gifts.

Each moment is a gift.

Open your eyes and see, your ears and hear.

Abundance and gifts surround you, always.

Love is all

Life's Journey

The path to the goal is not always so clear,
There are side paths which may distract you
At times it will seem your vision
is all but non-existent
You can not always see the miracles of
creation that are under your feet,
If you are lead astray in another direction be
open to the purpose of that direction,
Be it, a little more knowledge, or
someone to meet along the way.
Never give up on what you truly know and believe.
Hold fast to your dreams

T.B. HUMAN

Wisdom will prevail, never fear.

The mists will soon disappear,

And the scene will be breathtaking.

Take heed to listen to that small quiet voice

within before you leap into anything

The wheel of fortune is spinning your way,

Breathe deeply and enjoy the

beauty that surrounds you

If your shoes are too tight, go barefoot in the sun,

Life is a breeze when you have us on your side,

In love light and laughter.

FEATHERS IN THE MIST

As a bird flies,

Single and free,

I fly, homeward.

My soul supports me on my journey,

Onward ever onward

Time of visions end is near.

All is to be as in day's gone bye,

Things of this earth,

All shall vanish into dust.

But immortal beings we all persist,

Ever growing in consciousness of ONE.

Relationship wisdom

When people fall in love they tell each
other what they like about each other.

When they fall out of love they tell
each other what they do not like

And that is the only thing that changes
Its that simple.

True Love

True love will always lift you up

It will not tare you down.

It does not point out your faults,

Rather, it encourages your strengths.

Think on this dear one.

Go with the grace of God's love to care for thee,

Be gentle upon yourself, all is well

All is love

You can not separate from that which is yourself

Trust!

There is always a time of action,

And, a time to be still.

It's only a wise man who knows the difference.

The wakefulness of the universe is

likened to a sleeping child,

It dreams unaware of the

catastrophes that surround it

Nestled softly in the bosom of unconsciousness.

As the child grows, so it experiences fear,

Fear of the unknown,

Fear of the dark,

Until one by one it conquers its fears.

Finally, at adulthood it trusts its

knowledge and tests its reality,

And in doing so strengthening

its knowing of all that is.

FEATHERS IN THE MIST

If you think I would ever hurt you,

You know me not at all,

If you think I would ever leave you,

Not even if the sky would fall.

For you are my love forever more.

T.B. HUMAN

Remember, the old must give way to the new,
The new can not manifest if we hang on to the old.

Change is not bad, it is merely change.

Good – bad, who knows?
It is a matter of perception.

You can either see the beautiful flowers in the garden
Or
See only the spiders, bees and other
things that cause harm
It is your choice what you focus upon
Think upon that.

FEATHERS IN THE MIST

We will be always near, never fear child

We will not desert you, no matter what

Do not fear to make mistakes,

For he who never made a mistake,

never learnt to grow

And he who never dared, never succeeded.

Be at peace, God Speed your

journey into understanding.

T.B. HUMAN

The Universe is unfolding to you child of light,

Dear one, we love and guide you well

It is only in a state of love and thankfulness

that we can guide you

FEATHERS IN THE MIST

Emotional attachments float away,

As we learn to love a little more each day.

We learn not to cause ourselves such pain,

No more the struggle, that has been in vain.

The tide has turned and the water falls,

However, many will hear the call.

The call to home to be as one,

And soon your job will be well done.

Shine out my love for all to see,

Shine out for the love of humanity.

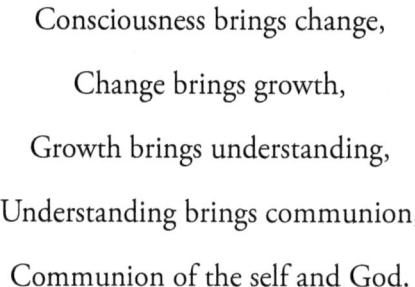

Consciousness brings change,

Change brings growth,

Growth brings understanding,

Understanding brings communion,

Communion of the self and God.

The way to teach your children

Is

To reward the trying

Not punish for the results.

Encourage their joy

If you are not happy with your life

Then it's simple

Change it!

WHAT I NEED TO KNOW

Know yourself that is all,
Know your weakness for what they are, simply that.

Be master of your self, overcome fear.
Do not give it a place within your heart.

Live life that's full of Grace.
Be strong inside and win the race.

Know yourself, look hard and fast,
Look honestly in that looking glass.

Know all that is was of your own making.
Accept this, and see where the ground is shaking.

T.B. HUMAN

Once upon a midsummer's morn,

A lass of finery was born,

Walked the lane of life once more,

Searching for one too adore.

Put things right this time my love,

Was the message from above!

Give to feelings running deep,

Is the father who our soul does keep.

Keeps the life of humanity a flow,

As gently onward we do go.

Be guided by what you know is right,

Be true now with all your might.

Or your soul will morn and wail,

And never more to lift the veil.

FEATHERS IN THE MIST

Flow on smoothly with the tide,

Allow the love to no longer hide.

It is strength above all others.

Listen deeply to the call,

For it is for one and all.

One can only be the light, when in a state of peace.

Peace is self love and contentment.

Never wanting more than you have,

Understand you will always have enough.

This applies to all things.

You are surrounded by love,

Yet most of you cast it aside for a distant misery.

Wake up and live the fullness that is eternal spirit.

If you do not see love, then be sure

that the fault is your own.

It may be that what you do see as love is an illusion.

If you give of unconditional love,

then you are nourished from within

the very essence of your being.

For always so you give, you receive.

Love is a tool by which we learn.

And ultimately, we learn,

We must not imprison with love,

For if we are guilty of this,

We will never find true love.

T.B. HUMAN

Go softly on your way,

And to me Lord Jesus softly pray,

That peace will reign, and hope will lead,

That wisdom and strength, will now proceed

That love will grow with each new day,

And truth be seen in every way,

Life's an illusion, now you see.

What true souls have been sent to thee.

Many friends now gather round,

Be grateful that you they have found.

Found before they feel the blast,

All one day will feel at last.

FEATHERS IN THE MIST

The time is swift approaching now,

When man shall know the truth somehow

We all are same under the skin

And love connects us all within.

T.B. HUMAN

Out of chaos comes a deeper sense of clarity,

Out of restlessness comes a deeper sense of peace.

One can not journey into the light unless

it is by the way of the darkness.

All must be experienced and

accepted to find the ultimate,

Peace of God within.

In that space we find that God and Self are one.

It is only our creative power that wields the sword,

To cut through old ways,

Healing perceptions and misconceptions.

For in truth, all is God.

We are but expressions of that divinity.

It's time to accept Grace by which we stand,

And be a light unto the universe of darkness.

Go forth in the light of God that is yourself.

Peace be with you.

T.B. HUMAN

Child be at peace.

Know we love and care for thee,

Feel our love surround you like a velvet cloak.

Be sure we give you all you need.

Know this,

It is only for you to ask, and it is done.

If it be the fathers will.

It can only be for thee,

You can not awaken the world on your own.

Know that we bring the changes

only when need bee.

All is planned, down to the finest

detail of perfection.

We do not allow too many memories of the past,

But in time you will remember, your true heritage.

But not yet.

You must grow comfortable in your knowledge,

then expand.

Bring your knowledge into your daily life,

Live and love the teachings as you know them.

Service, always service.

T.B. HUMAN

If I could find my purpose,

Then I would have the world.

But to find it,

I must first find what it is not.

FEATHERS IN THE MIST

For those who stand at the gate and wait,

Enter now though Gods narrow gate,

And walk the razor-edged path.

The path of hope for all to follow,

Know there will be a bright tomorrow.

Today's shadows will soon disappear,

A time for laughter and no more tears.

Know your race has been well run,

Accept your place now with the son.

For all things that have been,

Let go forever.

Shine out for all to see.

Show that darkness can no longer touch thee.

Feel the gossamer wings at your back.

Know the truth and you will never lack.

Trust is,

Believing in the creation of this moment.

Forever is now.

I reached a hand up to the father,

Asking for guidance,

And it was given.

It's just sometimes,

I did not recognize the gift.

Love remembered but not found,

Why is it to this love I am bound.

Invisible strings pulling strong,

Where oh where do I belong.

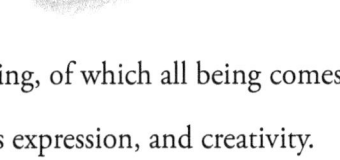

Love is a feeling, of which all being comes,

Love seeks expression, and creativity.

If you limit love to the expression of sexuality,

You will limit growth.

It is but a part of loves expression,

But not it's limit.

Gently with the strength of God go I,

Forward ever forward into the unknown

Trusting each step is placed on solid ground.

Learning to live for this day, and its blessings

If I dare look back, or forward, I loose.

For I have learnt the secret is to live in this moment

And in that I have found everlasting peace.

FEATHERS IN THE MIST

Dark shadows, flashing in the night,

Soft shadows echo, bringing fright.

Love yourself child, set your self free.

Free of fear, fear of lack,

Remember now in times of lack,

That love, and peace connect all things

And these will draw with invisible strings

Pulling all you need to you,

And this will be in all you do

Attraction is the key you see,

For every experience sent to thee.

T.B. HUMAN

Take the golden rose in your hand,

It brings with it love straight from the man (Jesus),

Time to cut old strings that bind,

And leave all the weight behind.

Love self, set your self free.

That is all, we ask of thee.

Once the self is filled with love,

Blessings can flow from up above.

Abundance of all things flowing through,

Supporting your in all you do.

Magic, is the price for facing fear,

Setting self free from all its chains,

That holds the soul from all its claims.

Do as you think,

Be as you feel,

And all will be well with your world and you.

T.B. HUMAN

Look about you, blue eyes,

Look to the love about you.

We wrap you in the finest cloak of silk,

Angels tend to your every need.

Feel in your heart the gifts we have been given,

Magnificent in their simplicity.

Others now will overlook them,

For they are for your eyes to see,

Rest gently with our arms about you,

Know our love will ever flow.

In a cloak that will surround you,

As on your journey you will go.

Gather to your heart the beauty,

FEATHERS IN THE MIST

Give love to all who come to thee,

Be as we are gentle lady,

For you, life has just begun.

Know not one thing in your life is lacking,

Just ask and it will be given,

For you the gift is and will be.

Gods Grace and love it will surround you,

Be love that is all we need.

T.B. HUMAN

Birds take flight on silent wings.

Soaring high, towards the morning sun.

Each alone but together.

So, it should be with you, little one.

Walk on your own two feet,

no need to lean on any one.

There will be times when you need to stop and rest,

And rest your head on a caring chest.

Gather to yourself the wisdom,

Experience brings a higher truth.

Catch the feathers in the mist,

These will lead you home.

FEATHERS IN THE MIST

Mirror, mirror who's that I see,

Looking through the eyes, looking back at me.

Am I a dream?

Or am I the one that is real?

Is it the mirror face considering its own reflection?

Which one is real?

The answer came on boldly through,

It's I who's real looking back at you.

But what of me here, am I not real?

No, there is more than one of you.

Other dimensions, flowing through.

We all exist within the same space,

There is no future or no past

When looking in the looking glass.

Faces forming changing floating bye,

T.B. HUMAN

Do they see my face in quest?
Do they search for what is best?
Do they too long to find their
missing links, catch glimpses,
Feelings breaking through.

Understandings come for now you see,
I can accept that there is more than one of me!

Long ago and far away,

Dancing figures, in another way.

Circling light, flowing bright.

Joy in being, joy in life.

Spirit of truth shine on,

Through the long dark night.

T.B. HUMAN

We become defensive when we are afraid,

We become afraid when we do not understand,

The solution is to stop judgment,

and be open to listening

There are many truths in this world

And they all are dependant upon the corner

of the room you are sitting in at that time.

People fear what they do not understand,

As it threatens their position in the world

If there is more to the world than they know

Then it means they are wrong

People do not like to be wrong.

FEATHERS IN THE MIST

I walk a road that can only be traveled by me

On that road I encounter the

reflections of everything I believe

If I am blessed,

I will soon discover that all I believe is illusion

If I am blessed,

Each belief will swiftly change

and grow into a new belief

If I am blessed,

I will swiftly transform my life from

one of fear and ignorance

To a life of trust, faith, hope and charity

All of which will be the vehicle for the

journey of the next stage of my life.

T.B. HUMAN

Children of the world unite,

Regardless of color black or white.

Time is swift approaching now,

To recognize the truth somehow.

Truth that there is one God for all,

But he lives inside of thee.

If you accept this precious gift,

And let his love come shining through,

Reach out to all with helping hand.

Give always Hope, so others too may stand.

Stand for truth, and trust and right.

Helping others always in their plight.

Judge not one man on earth,

It is for him to judge his own worth.

Walk beside him as a friend,

And this will be until the very end.

FEATHERS IN THE MIST

Very soon well turn the tide,

That be the tide of discontent, for

that was never what was meant.

Live in laughter every day,

When at work and when at play,

Be happy no matter what is your lot.

After all, in truth you asked for what you've got.

T.B. HUMAN

If you're not happy,

Change it!

FEATHERS IN THE MIST

Something is hard only when it is not meant to be,

It may not be time.

Let it go, and if it is meant to

come back to you it will.

When you are using your intuition,

your life becomes a journey

Not a struggle.

If you're struggling, it's because you are

not listening to that small quiet voice.

You are not in tune.

The higher self or god self manifests only

the finest experience for you to learn by.

All too often we hold onto

something, be it a way of life,

a belief, or a dream out of fear of lack.

Remember that the new can not manifest

if you are hanging on to the old.

So, take a big breath and let go,

and surrender to God.

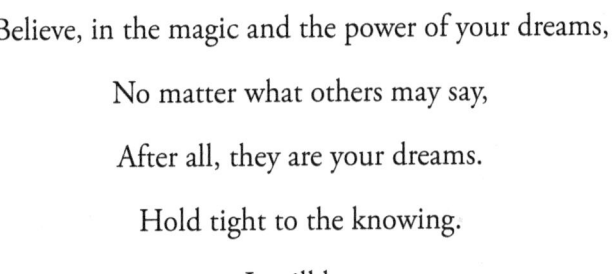

Believe, in the magic and the power of your dreams,

No matter what others may say,

After all, they are your dreams.

Hold tight to the knowing.

It will be.

T.B. HUMAN

Look into the eyes my child and
you will see the truth,
It is one place that man can not hide,
Behind the sadness and the lies.

All he thinks and fears and knows,
Will all be there in the eyes to show.

See the love and kindness too,
All his virtues showing through.

Look into the eyes and see
What truth there is for humanity!

CODE OF ENLIGHTENMENT

Be happy, always.

Do not get caught up in the negative turmoil.

Neither the imaginings of the future

nor dwell upon the past.

Steer clear of any conversations that

will cause another harm.

Look for the good in all, and give them praise.

Let your hope for the future shine

forth like a lantern for all to see.

Make a little time for yourself everyday.

If someone wishes to talk with you, listen.

You need not comment, for he will

hear his own realizations

Mirrored within his own words.

T.B. HUMAN

Know you are no better or no

worse than any other man.

Live in abundance by focusing on what you do have,

rather than what you do not.

By dwelling upon lack you will surely

create it within your life

And consciousness, and will be unhappy.

Above all,

Remember, we learn and grow to

become awakened spirit.

To one day become fully conscious

light beings, living within a

Framework of unconditional love.

There is more than one rose in the garden.

Why do you limit yourself to the beauty of just one?

Look at all the other blossoms,

You are surrounded by their beauty,

If you would just take time to look.

True wealth is happiness of the soul,

This can not be measured,

Stored, hoarded or stolen,

Unless we allow it to be.

Be happy little one,

Let your joy fill the universe with light,

So all may see and follow,

Without you saying one single word.

Just by being.

FEATHERS IN THE MIST

Mists rise with the early morning sun,

Soon to disappear in the light of full day.

Soon the mists will disappear,

A time of laughter no more tears.

Gather your understanding to your soul.

You will recognize the truth somehow.

Know the power of your thoughts.

Build a world that is full and bright,

Build now with hope and all your might.

T.B. HUMAN

Take what of knowledge as a whole,

Do just as you would,

Be now aware of what influences you

have created within your reality.

Look at them for what they truly are, illusions.

See the wisdom in standing aside,

Let the tide rise and fall,

For tomorrow, just as surely as the sun will rise,

The spirit of man will seek and

grow in understanding.

Be yea of faith and strong heart.

And all will be well.

FEATHERS IN THE MIST

Now the mists have disappeared,

Feathers of knowledge gathered to my soul.

The sun shines brighter than before,

And a new world unfolds at my fingertips.

I found the love lost so long ago,

Finally I found that illusive key.

That illusive love you see,

Is me!

T.B. HUMAN

Be ever full in this moment,

This is eternity.

ABOUT THE AUTHOR:

T.B. HUMAN – Writer, author, speaker and presenter. A businesswoman and entrepreneur. T.B Human writes about the insights gathered from real life experience of allowing herself to be human. Her own journey into healing her life became the catalyst for what was to develop over 30years to become her life's work into healing.

Having dedicated her life to developing practical tools, which support the development of people's ability to cope with life from an empowered perspective no matter what their history or circumstances.

T.B. HUMAN is a woman who has achieved a great deal armed with nothing other than Faith, Truth, Self-belief and Determination. Unafraid to challenge the rules and limits of society, she walks a path where angels fear to tread. Pushing forward believing that every person has the potential to create an abundant fulfilling life; she inspires all who meet her.

In her work she discovered that it was rare to find anything which supported people to simply be human. New-Age books and programs just didn't help her or others to really change their lives. They seemed to be just a placebo, there had to be something more, something that empowered people from within. She set out to discover how the human psyche developed over a lifetime and how we as individuals evolved. The result of the 30 years of discovery and dedication is the product range of TRUITY, Games, Books and Workbooks.

Today T.B. HUMAN is a mother and grandmother having lived an amazing life, overcoming cancer four times, and surviving what most would crumble and give up.

Fiercely passionate about issues which involve the empowerment and safety of people of all cultures. All in all, T.B. HUMAN is a woman of substance and very, very real

www.ingramcontent.com/pod-product-compliance
Lightning Source LLC
Chambersburg PA
CBHW070653050426
42451CB00008B/331